The Costs
of Immigration
to Taxpayers

Analytical and
Policy Issues

Georges Vernez

Kevin F. McCarthy

Supported by
The Ford Foundation and the
James Irvine Foundation

RAND

PREFACE

In the midst of steady increases in international immigration and a sluggish national economy, the question of whether immigrants fully pay—in the form of taxes—for the public services they use is being hotly contested by analysts and policymakers alike. This report reviews the recent estimates of net costs of immigration that have fueled this debate. It identifies the reasons that they differ so widely and outlines what it would take to develop more reliable estimates. It is part of a comprehensive study of the effects of 30 years of immigration on the state of California and was funded by The Ford Foundation and the James Irvine Foundation.

This study should be of special interest to policymakers; federal, state, and local officials; advocates; and researchers concerned with gaining a better understanding of the complexities of the effects of immigration on U.S. society.

CONTENTS

FIGURE

Do immigrants contribute more to public revenues than they receive in benefits from public services? Do state and local governments pay a disproportionate share of the cost of services used by immigrants? These two questions have received considerable analytical and political attention in recent years because of a rapid growth in the number of immigrants, their high concentration in a few states, and a lagging economy that has slowed growth in public revenues. This report reviews the estimates of the net fiscal costs of immigration made by several recent and well publicized studies—at the national, state, and local levels. We asked why these estimates differ so widely and what should be done to develop more credible estimates.

FINDINGS OF RECENT STUDIES

The studies included in this review were selected because they were completed after 1990, sought to be comprehensive in their coverage of services used and public contributions made by immigrants, and were the latest "best" estimates made by authors or institutions.[1] Nearly all of these studies build on the pioneering study prepared in 1992 for the Los Angeles County Board of Supervisors, which is among those reviewed here.

The studies tend to agree on only one thing: immigrants' relative contributions to public revenues. Specifically, there is general

---

[1]Several authors or institutions made multiple estimates, then "improved" subsequent estimates.

agreement that, currently, illegal immigrants contribute less to public revenues than do those who were amnestied under the Immigration Reform and Control Act of 1986 (IRCA). They, in turn, contribute less than legal immigrants, who contribute less than the native-borns. This finding merely reflects differences in the average incomes of these various groups rather than in their immigration status per se. In short, the suggestive finding that illegal immigrants are net consumers of public services is more a product of their low incomes than of their immigration status.

Otherwise, and in spite of their common basis, the findings of these studies differ widely. For example, estimates of the yearly per-capita costs of providing federal, state, and local services to immigrants range from a low of $2,638 to a high of $4,476. Similarly, yearly per-capita revenue estimates vary from $1,051 to $3,644. Overall, the net cost estimates range from a yearly "surplus" of $1,400 per immigrant to a "deficit" of $1,600.

There are two main reasons for these disagreements and, hence, for the absence of a reliable estimate of the actual net public costs (benefits) of illegal immigrants or of immigrants as a whole. First, the data needed to make detailed cost/benefit calculations are unavailable. This lack of data forces each study to make assumptions about immigrants' service usage and revenue contributions—assumptions that are often mistaken. Second, studies differ in the range of public services and revenue sources they include and on a variety of other complex conceptual issues ranging from how to define an immigrant to how to measure costs.

DATA NEEDS

Accurate, reliable, and comparable estimates of the net fiscal costs of immigration require several different types of information:

- An accurate count of immigrants by immigration status and other relevant socioeconomic characteristics.

- Reliable information on immigrants' *actual* use of all relevant services and the *actual* public costs of providing those services to immigrants and members of their families, differentiated by immigration status.

• Reliable information on which revenue sources immigrants *actually* contribute to and the *actual* amount of their contributions, again differentiated by immigration status.

In the absence of reliable data on these critical parameters, studies have made differing assumptions about the number of immigrants, their service usage, and their contributions to public revenues. Inaccurate assumptions can affect not only the magnitude of the estimates but also the direction of the net cost estimates.

Most studies, for example, assumed that immigrants' use of services is proportional to their numbers, regardless of their socioeconomic and immigration status. However, RAND data collected from a 1991 sample of Salvadoran and Filipino immigrants residing in Los Angeles challenge this proportionality assumption. Overall, our data suggest that use of public services is generally not affected by immigration status, including illegal status. It is affected by family income and family composition, particularly the presence of children under age five. In addition, immigrants' use of certain services such as libraries, public transit, parks, and recreation, is affected by a range of factors—income, number of children, and English proficiency—that condition the immigrants' need for the services.

Another common assumption made in these studies is that the incidence of tax payments and payroll deduction is uniformly high across income levels and immigration status. Our data suggest, to the contrary, that payroll deductions and federal tax filings vary significantly with immigration status—illegal immigrants have the lowest incidence of payroll tax deducted and the lowest incidence of federal and state income tax filing.

Without additional data on service usage and revenues, the question of how much immigrants actually cost the public treasury cannot be answered. A recent RAND pilot survey of immigrants concluded that it would be feasible to collect such data by immigration status, but that it would be expensive: up to $7 million for a survey of 9,000 immigrants in nine sites across the country.[2]

---

[2]Julie DaVanzo, Jennifer Hawes-Dawson, R. Burciaga Valdez, Georges Vernez, *Surveying Immigrant Communities: Policy Imperatives and Technical Challenges*, Santa Monica, Calif.: RAND, MR-247-FF, 1994.

A NEED FOR UNIFORM ACCOUNTING FRAMEWORK

Another fundamental reason for disagreement on the size of the net fiscal deficit or surplus caused by immigration is that analysts have not yet agreed on a *uniform accounting framework* for determining (a) which public services and which revenues, hence costs, ought to be included in estimating the costs of immigration; (b) how to define and categorize immigrants; and (c) how to select the appropriate accounting unit and measure costs, and over which period of time. The resolution of these issues will have a significant impact not only on the outcomes of future studies, but on their interpretation for policy.

Services to Be Included

A starting premise of any fiscal cost accounting framework is that all public services should be included or a justification provided for excluding a particular service. This has not, however, been the common practice: The range of public outlays has varied from a low of 40 percent to a high of 80 percent. While most studies agree that all services provided directly to individuals (e.g., education, nutrition, and social services) should be included, very few, if any, studies include such major categories of federal expenditures as national defense, support of research and development, general government and administrative expenditures, and interest on the national debt.

Such exclusion may be justified on one of two grounds—neither of which fully hold. Either immigrants do not derive any benefit from these services or the marginal costs of providing these services to immigrants is zero. The former assumption is questionable at best, and the latter assumption—even if closer to reality—implicitly suggests that native-born residents should subsidize the provision of these services to immigrants.

Social insurance programs such as Social Security present another source of accounting disagreements. The implicit argument for their exclusion is that these programs are self-funded. But these programs often have a redistributive function that provides disproportionate benefits to low-income immigrants and natives. In addition, the revenues from the special funds are often treated as general revenues.

Even when the decision is made to include social insurance expenditures in the cost estimates, there is still a decision as to whether those costs should be allocated on a current, intergenerational, or even a lifetime basis. Because most immigrants are young and thus will not be eligible to receive social insurance benefits for several years, the cost allocation approach that is used can result in as much as a tenfold difference in the estimates of these costs.

Revenues to Be Included

Just as all services should be included on the cost side of the ledger, so should all revenues be included on the benefit side. But once again, this has not been the common practice, and the public revenues included in these studies can range from a low of 45 percent of total public revenues to a high of 75 percent. Revenues collected from individuals (e.g., personal income, property, and sales taxes) have generally been included. But revenues from businesses, banks, and corporations have typically been excluded. Exclusion of corporate and commercial property taxes is especially problematic when the full costs of the local services provided to business are attributed to consumers, including immigrants, as has typically been the case. It leads to an overestimate of service costs attributed to immigrants or, alternatively, to an underestimate of the revenues deemed attributable to them.

Defining Who Is an "Immigrant"

All studies agreed that *foreign-born noncitizens* should be classified as immigrants. But they disagreed about how to treat naturalized immigrants (those who have become citizens) and the native-born children of illegal and legal immigrants. Naturalized immigrants and native-born children of immigrants are, by U.S. law, citizens, and from a legal perspective they are not immigrants. However, had they or their parents not immigrated to the United States, they would not be in the country in the first place: Thus, from a pragmatic perspective, it is arguable that they should be counted with immigrants for cost accounting purposes.

Categorizing Immigrants

The categories used to group immigrants are important not only to the estimation procedures but also for the policy implications that can be drawn from these estimates. Some studies have generally grouped immigrants into three categories: currently illegal, those who received amnesty, and other immigrants. Other studies just focused on immigrants as an aggregate category. Since most estimates rely on assumptions about average incomes and service usage within the subgroups of immigrants they identify, these estimates depend directly upon which groupings are used. Just as important, forecasts about the future that are drawn from these estimates hinge on how immigrants are categorized. Typically, the implicit assumption built into these studies is that if a particular group currently produces a net public "deficit," then future immigration by that group either ought to be eliminated or reduced.

In fact, such broad groupings fail to capture the diversity of immigrants or to provide an adequate basis for policy, because they do not mirror the criteria used to admit legal immigrants. More appropriate categories would distinguish immigrants based on the determinants currently used to admit permanent immigrants, such as refugee status, family reunification, employment, or other more specific characteristics that would provide a better determinant of whether immigrants are likely to be high or low consumers of public services, or revenue generators.

Defining the Appropriate Accounting Unit

The studies reviewed here allocated the costs of services to individual immigrants but measured revenue contributions on the basis of families, where the "immigration status" of the family is defined in terms of the status of the family head. This inconsistency in accounting units poses a problem for families containing a mixture of native and foreign-born members or members whose immigration status's differ—a frequent occurrence.

Lifetime Versus Annual Costs

All studies reviewed have focused on the net fiscal costs of immigration in a given year. This is an appropriate perspective if the concern is with balancing government budgets from one year to the next. However, immigrants' use of services and contributions to revenues are likely to vary over time as the immigrants become more familiar with U.S. society and labor markets. Indeed, the services provided to immigrants, especially education and health services, can appropriately be regarded as investments made today in expectation of a return to be received tomorrow. From this perspective, the appropriate question is not whether the "net costs" of providing services to immigrants yield a "surplus" or a "deficit" on an annual basis but whether, over the duration of the immigrant's residence in the United States, the nation reaps a net cost or benefit. None of the studies reviewed considered this issue.

RECASTING THE POLICY DEBATE

In spite of their proliferation, recent studies on the net fiscal costs of immigration do not provide a reliable estimate of what those net costs are. Moreover, without new data and agreement on a uniform accounting framework, additional studies will likely not provide a definitive answer to the policy questions raised about the costs of immigration.

Despite their limitations, recent studies of the costs of immigration have focused attention on a heretofore overlooked issue—whether the public costs of immigration should be considered in formulating the nation's immigration policy. To date, such central immigration policy issues as how many and which immigrants to admit and what public services they should be offered have been formulated without a consideration of their fiscal implications. Instead, they have been determined by long-term economic, humanitarian, and social considerations. Incorporating fiscal considerations in the public policy calculus would represent a real departure from past practice.

Considering public costs in immigration policy should redirect the current debate away from a focus on the aggregate public costs of immigration—and hence, away from aggregate numbers exclusively. After all, we do not expect the native population, any subgroup of the native-born, or the nation as a whole to "fully pay its way" on a yearly basis, as our continuing federal budget deficit bears witness. Instead, the debate should refocus on the individual and family factors that lead to high or low public service usage and the economic success of immigrants, not just in a single year, but over the entire course of their residence in the United States. In short, the policy debate should be refocused on the question of the selectivity of immigrants and on the costs and benefits immigrants generate over the long term, not just the short term, which seems to have been the focus to date.

ACKNOWLEDGMENTS

The coauthors of this report collaborated closely in its writing. We thank the participants in a RAND workshop titled "The Public Costs of Immigration: Why Does it Matter?" held on January 26, 1995, for the many insights they provided on the analytical and interpretation issues raised in studying the fiscal costs of immigration. We also thank our RAND colleagues Julie DaVanzo and Robert Schoeni for their comments on earlier drafts. Karla McAffee provided skillful assistance in preparing this manuscript.

Chapter One

INTRODUCTION

BACKGROUND

The question of whether immigration generates more costs than benefits for the nation has emerged as a major public issue in recent years as a result of several developments: First, the number of immigrants who have entered the country during the last decade rivals that at the beginning of the century when immigration was at its peak. Second, these immigrants are concentrated in a few states—California, Florida, Illinois, New York, and Texas—and in such large metropolitan areas as Los Angeles, Miami, New York, and Chicago within those states. For instance, two out of five residents in Los Angeles today are foreign-born. Third, although today's immigrants come from all parts of the world, the vast majority come either from Mexico and Central America on the one hand or Asia on the other. Fourth, the country is experiencing major economic and social changes made worse by a deep and lengthy recession that began in 1990. These changes include major cuts in defense expenditures, restructuring of the economy in response to heightened international competition, slow employment growth, and an unwillingness among the electorate to tax itself to support public service programs. Nowhere have these changes been felt more strongly than in California, where the nation's highest immigration rates have coincided with a deep and long recession. California voters' passage in 1994 of Proposition 187, which would deny illegal aliens access to social, health, and education public benefits, is only one manifestation of a new social climate.

In this new climate, immigration and immigrants have been singled out as major contributors to the growth in demands placed on public programs and services, and thus to the budgetary deficits that several states and localities have had to confront in recent years. Unable to raise public revenues through increased taxes, and required by law to balance their budgets, states and localities have had no alternative but to cut the level of benefits they provided to all their residents.

Immigrants, like citizens, however, not only consume public services; they also pay taxes. As a result, two questions currently dominate the immigration policy debate:

1. Do immigrants' contributions to public revenues cover the costs of the public services they receive?

2. What is the *net* budgetary cost (or benefit) to states and localities of providing services to immigrants, and to illegal immigrants in particular?

While the first question is the object of attention both in the United States and in other western nations currently experiencing high levels of immigration, the second is unique to our federal form of government. The three different levels of government—federal, state, and local—are responsible for the financing and/or delivery of different kinds of services. The lower levels of government are principally responsible for education and protective services—police and fire— and share with the federal government in the costs of providing health and welfare services. Immigration, although a federal responsibility, may place a disproportionate demand on those services provided by state and local governments, thus generating a possible imbalance in cost-sharing (Vernez, 1993).

Several recent studies have addressed these two questions. Their findings, however, differ so widely that policymakers and the general public are understandably confused as to what to believe. For example, national estimates of the effects of immigration on the public treasury reported in the media and circulating in policymaking circles differ by as much as $67 billion—ranging from a $25 billion annual surplus to a $42 billion annual deficit.

PURPOSE OF THIS STUDY

This report reviews national and local studies estimating the fiscal effects of immigration on state and local governments. Although there are many reasons why they differ so widely, the single most important reason is that the data necessary to reliably measure public costs and revenues are not currently available. As a result, all studies are forced to rely on estimates, and those estimates vary significantly in the services and revenues they include, and in the variables, behavioral assumptions, and methodologies they use. In addition, they sometimes differ in the policy or analytical questions they seek to answer and hence in how they categorize subgroups of immigrants, how they treat the citizen children of immigrants, and in how they allocate costs and revenues to immigrants.

The way these issues are addressed can predetermine a study's outcome. But these issues are secondary to a more basic question: What is the point of these studies in the first place? Why, for example, should we expect all immigrants, or any particular subgroup of immigrants, to "fully pay their way"? We don't expect it of natives, or any subgroup of the native-born, nor even of the nation as a whole— as our continuing federal budget deficit bears witness.

There are several potential goals of these studies: First, to help determine whether the nation ought to close the door or open it more widely to new immigrants; second, to help determine how many immigrants the nation can afford to accept at any one time; third, to help determine which immigrants we want to let in and which we want to keep out; and fourth, to determine whether state and local jurisdictions ought to be compensated for the "excess" costs of providing services to illegal or other immigrants and by how much.

The policy questions that motivate the concern with the fiscal costs of immigration will shape a study's design and eventually its findings. Studies that nominally address the question of public costs and revenues, but that explicitly or implicitly address different policy questions, will not be readily comparable.

ORGANIZATION OF THIS REPORT

The remainder of this report is divided into three chapters. The first reviews the findings of recent studies. The second discusses the key conceptual issues, behavioral assumptions, and cost allocation rules on which we need to reach consensus if we are to improve the reliability and comparability of estimates of the public costs of immigration. The third outlines the range of policy questions that these studies, appropriately redesigned and supported by newly collected data, can help address.

Chapter Two

REVIEW OF RECENT STUDIES

The number of studies addressing the question of the public costs of immigration has increased in recent years. In this chapter, we summarize their findings, identify points of agreement and disagreement, and outline the main reasons for disagreements.

SELECTION OF STUDIES

The studies included in this review were selected according to three criteria. First, they must have been completed after 1990. Prior studies were reviewed in Eric Rothman and Thomas Espenshade's "Fiscal Impacts of Immigration to the United States."[1] They found that these earlier studies do not answer the question of the net fiscal costs of immigration but suggest that the fiscal burden of serving immigrants falls more heavily on states and localities than on the federal government (p. 412).

Second, we included only studies that sought to be comprehensive in their coverage of immigrants' service usage and public contributions. Thus, studies focusing on a single or limited set of programs such as Aid to Families with Dependent Children (AFDC), or a single country of origin (e.g., Mexico), were excluded.

Finally, only the latest, and hence, the "best" estimates made by authors or institutions were reviewed. Over the years, several authors have made repeated estimates and "improved" subsequent esti-

---

[1]Eric S. Rothman and Thomas J. Espenshade, 1992.

5

mates based on additional information or in response to criticisms raised by others. Including these earlier estimates in this review would not add to our understanding of the issues.[2]

RELATIONSHIPS AMONG STUDIES

The key characteristics of the studies that met these criteria, including the reasons they were undertaken and their findings, are summarized in Table 1. Two preliminary observations can be made about this set of studies that broadly identify their limitations. The first relates to their charters. Several studies were requested by state or local governmental bodies seeking to make a case for fiscal relief; others were sponsored by advocacy groups in response to prior studies. While these charters did not necessarily undermine the objectivity of the estimates, they did require the researchers to employ existing data, regardless of their adequacy, and to focus on specific subgroups of immigrants, mostly recent immigrants.

Second, six of the studies are not independent of one another, as shown in Figure 1. One or another aspect of their estimates relies on the "pioneering" study prepared in 1992 for the Los Angeles County Board of Supervisors by the Los Angeles County Internal Services Division (ISD, 1992). These studies either take the ISD study's estimates for Los Angeles and extrapolate them to the nation (Huddle, 1993), or they endeavor to partially "improve" on the income assumptions, service cost coverage, or overall methodology it used (Clark and Passel, 1993; Passel, 1994; Romero, Chang, and Parker, 1994; and Center for Immigration Studies (CIS), 1994). Indeed, most of the debate on the fiscal costs of immigration over the past three years has focused on refining or responding to charges and countercharges about one or another aspect of this original study.

---

[2]The only exception concerns Huddle's latest reestimate of the national costs of immigration for 1993. The methodology for his yearly update does not differ from that of his 1992 estimate used in this study, with one exception. The 1993 estimate includes Social Security contributions and government outlays. He estimates the net cost of Social Security to immigrants to have been $1.4 billion.

Table 1

Key Characteristics of Studies Reviewed

Author(s)	Year of Estimate	Requestor	Jurisdiction for Which Costs (Benefits) Were Estimated	Motivation	Subgroups Included (Number in Millions)	Net Fiscal Surplus/ Deficit per Capita (Dollars)	Displacement Multiplier Effect Included
Internal Services Division, 1992	FY92	Board of Supervisors, Los Angeles County	County	Request federal assistance	Native-born (6.9) Illegal immigrants (.70)[a] Amnestied immigrants (.72) Post-1980 legal immigrants (.63) Total immigrants (2.05)	−146 −402 −204 −256 −293	No
Huddle, 1993	FY92	Carrying Capacity Network	Aggregate federal, state, and local	Determine net fiscal effect	Native-born Illegal immigrants Citizen children of illegal immigrants Amnestied immigrants (2.5) Post-1970 legal immigrants (12.0) Total immigrants (19.3)	+178 −1,584 −1,342 −1,627 −1,587	Yes
Clark and Passel, 1993	FY92	Author-initiated	County	Critique tax payment estimates of ISD study	All post-1980 immigrants (1.53)	−230	No
Passel, 1994	FY92	The Tomás Rivera Center	Aggregate federal, state, and local	Critique and re-estimate of Huddle, 1993 study	Illegal immigrants (1.6) Amnestied immigrants (2.1) Post-1970 legal immigrants (9.8) Total immigrants (13.5)	−266 +616 +2,385 +1,488	No
Center for Immigration Studies, 1994	FY92	CIS-initiated	Aggregate federal, state, and local	Critique and re-estimate Huddle (1993) and Passel (1994)	All post-1970 immigrants (18.4)	−1,023	Yes

Table 1—continued

Author(s)	Year of Estimate	Requestor	Jurisdiction for Which Costs (Benefits) Were Estimated	Motivation	Subgroups Included (Number in Millions)	Net Fiscal Surplus/ Deficit per Capita (Dollars)	Displacement Multiplier Effect Included
Romero, Chang, and Parker, 1994	FY95	Governor's office, California	State	Request federal assistance	Illegal immigrants (1.7) Citizen children of illegal immigrants (.20)	-1,561	No
Parker and Rea, 1993	FY92	Special Committee on Border Issues, Calif. State Senate	State and local in San Diego County	Identify costs of illegal immigration	Illegal immigrants in San Diego (.22)	-465	No
King, 1994	FY80	Author-initiated	State of New Jersey	Determine net fiscal effect	Native-born All immigrants (.94)	-304 -304	No
King, 1994	FY80	Author-initiated	All local governments in New Jersey	Determine net fiscal effect	Native-born All immigrants (.94)	-125 -194	No

NOTE: See list of references for full citations of studies.

[a]250,000 citizen children of immigrants are not included.

RAND *MR705-1*

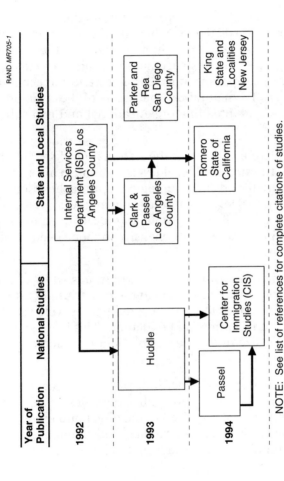

Year of Publication	National Studies	State and Local Studies
1992		Internal Services Department (ISD) Los Angeles County
1993	Huddle	Clark & Passel Los Angeles County / Romero State of California / Parker and Rea San Diego County
1994	Passel / Center for Immigration Studies (CIS)	King State and Localities New Jersey

NOTE: See list of references for complete citations of studies.

Figure 1—Studies Included in Our Review and Their Interrelationships

The independent studies (Parker and Rea, 1993; King, 1994) make no less a contribution to this genre of studies, but, for whatever reasons, have generally been ignored by the media and analysts alike.[3]

APPROACH TO COMPARISON OF FINDINGS

There are three significant differences among the studies reviewed here: the level of jurisdiction on which they focus, their estimates of the number of illegal and other immigrants, and the assumptions they make regarding the displacement or multiplier effects immigrants have on job opportunities, earnings, and the economy as a whole (Table 1). To "neutralize" the effects of these factors on our comparisons, we adopted one organizational and two substantive procedures.

First, we compare estimates at the national level separately from those made at the state and local levels. Although all studies share similar conceptual and methodological approaches, some issues raised at the national level are not relevant at lower levels of government and vice versa. Also, the state and local government studies have generally been more comprehensive in their coverage of public costs and revenues.

Second, the *estimates compared here are expressed in costs or revenues per capita.* We do this to avoid the disparities in estimates of total costs and revenues that can be amplified by wide variations in estimates of the total immigrant population. This is especially true of estimates of the size of the illegal population, which can differ by more than 50 percent (see Table 1).

Third, our comparisons consider only the *direct* fiscal costs of services used by immigrants and the public revenues raised from them. There is *disagreement* about whether the direct public costs and revenues generated by immigrants are alleviated or amplified by the dynamic effects immigrants may have on the economy and the job op-

---

[3]Subsequent to completion of a draft of this report, three additional studies were released: Clark et al., 1994; U.S. General Accounting Office, 1994; U.S. General Accounting Office, 1995. All three derive from the studies shown in Figure 1 and hence shed no additional light on the issues discussed in this report.

portunities and earnings of natives. For example, two studies (Huddle, 1993; CIS, 1994) assert that immigrants displace native-born workers, and that the costs of public assistance, unemployment compensation, and other support services to displaced natives should therefore be added to the fiscal costs of immigration. Others either ignore this issue or argue that immigration has a positive multiplier effect on the economy and the earnings of natives and thus reduces the fiscal cost of immigration by indirectly increasing public revenues raised from the native-born.

Finally, our explanation of differences among competing estimates focuses on the major factors that explain those differences. We do not discuss several minor issues that have a lesser effect on variations in estimates. There are, for example, variations among studies in the estimated annual costs of educating an immigrant child or incarcerating a convicted immigrant criminal. Such service cost variations are not reviewed systematically here.

COMPARISON OF NATIONAL STUDIES

Three studies (Huddle, 1993; Passel, 1994; and CIS, 1994) have estimated the net fiscal costs of providing public services to immigrants from a national perspective. In the absence of actual counts of immigrants by immigration status and of data on actual service use and revenue payments by individual immigrants and/or immigrant families, these studies used a variety of indirect measures and assumptions to estimate costs and revenues. To estimate gross costs, they first estimated the annual average cost of providing public assistance, education, and criminal justice services per recipient and then multiplied this average by the number of immigrants *estimated* to receive the service (actual counts of immigrants receiving a specific service are generally not available). On the revenue side, the studies generally estimated the distribution of immigrant households by income and age groupings and applied average per-capita tax rates— for income, property, and sales taxes—to each grouping after adjusting for the *estimated* incidence of tax filings and remittances sent out of the country. The latter adjustment is needed for estimating the sales tax because remittances are not subject to sales tax.

Table 2 compares the per-capita costs of providing federal, state, and local assistance services to immigrants and the federal, state, and

Table 2

Per-Capita Annual Costs of Public Services and Revenues by Immigration Status at the National Level, 1992

| | Studies | | | | | | | | |
| | Huddle '93 | | | Passel '94 | | | CIS '94 | | |
Immigration Status	Costs	Revenues	Ratio[a]	Costs	Revenues	Ratio[a]	Costs	Revenues	Ratio[a]
Immigrants									
Illegal	2,103	519	4.05	1,718[b]	1,452	1.44			
Amnestied	2,185	816	2.67	1,785[b]	2,401	.56			
Legal, 1970–1992	2,940	1,313	2.20	2,402[b]	4,787	.50			
All above	2,638	1,051	2.60	2,156	3,644	.59	4,476	3,453	1.30
Native-born	2,552	2,730	.93		4,924				
Percentage total service costs or revenues included[c]	40	45		55	75		80	75	

SOURCE: See list of references for full citations of studies.

NOTE: A blank means the data are not available or not applicable.

[a]Ratio of costs to revenues.

[b]The Urban Institute provides no independent estimates of these costs. To estimate these costs we multiplied Huddle's cost estimates for illegal immigrants, amnestied, and "permanent 1970–1992" by .82, the ratio of the Urban Institute estimate of costs for "all above" to Huddle's estimate of costs for "all above."

[c]Because of difficulties we had in identifying accurately the extent of coverage of each study, our estimates of coverage should be considered approximate.

local tax revenue per capita contributed by immigrants as estimated by Huddle (1993), Passel (1994), and CIS (1994). All estimates were for 1992. The first two studies provided separate estimates for three groups of immigrants: illegal, amnestied, and legal immigrants who entered the country after 1970. All three studies computed an average for the total of these three groups of immigrants. In these studies, immigrants who entered the country prior to 1970 were grouped with the native-born.[4]

The studies differ significantly in their estimates for immigrants as a whole. On the *costs* side, the CIS estimate of costs per capita is nearly twice as large as Huddle's: $4,476 versus $2,638 per immigrant. Passel does not make an independent estimate of costs, although he adjusts downward Huddle's estimated costs for some services—mainly education, county-provided services, and public assistance.

On the *revenue* side, the studies differ by an order of magnitude of one to three, Huddle being on the low end and Passel and CIS on the high end: $1,051 versus $3,644 and $3,453 per immigrant, respectively.

Comparing costs with tax contributions, the Huddle and CIS studies found that immigrants contribute *less* in taxes than they cost in services, Huddle estimating a deficit about 50 percent higher than CIS. Passel, on the other hand, estimated that immigrants as a group contribute more in revenues than they consume in services.

What explains these differences? Primarily, differing decisions as to which taxes are included on the revenue side and which public services are included on the cost side. On the *cost* side, the differences among Huddle, Passel, and CIS can be entirely attributed to CIS's including programs not included by Huddle: Social Security, supplemental Medicare, federal workers' and veterans' benefits, the

---

[4]The extent of the bias introduced by this decision is unknown. On the one hand, pre-1970 immigrants have been here longer and hence may have higher income than more recent immigrants. On the other hand, they are also older than recent immigrants and hence may be higher users of health, Social Security, and other services and entitlements.

earned income tax credit, highway fund, interest costs on immigrant benefits, and net city costs (see Table A.1 in the appendix).[5]

On the *revenue* side, Huddle's exclusion of Social Security, unemployment insurance, federal and state taxes on gasoline, and state vehicle license fees accounts for 55 and 48 percent of the difference between his estimate of revenues and those of Huddle and CIS, respectively. The balance is nearly fully accounted for by differences in estimates of revenues collected from income, sale, and property taxes caused by differences in immigrant incomes estimated by the three studies (see Table A.2 in the appendix). Lacking actual data on income of immigrants by immigration status, the studies make widely different assumptions in this regard.

In brief, the differences among the studies in the estimated net costs of immigration are primarily caused by (1) differing assumptions about the incomes of immigrants by immigration status and (2) conceptual disagreements on which services to include on the cost side and which revenues to include on the revenue side. Using federal, state, and local government revenues and expenditures from the national accounts, we estimate that Huddle included approximately 40 percent of total public expenditures and 45 percent of all public revenues compared with 80 percent and 75 percent, respectively, for CIS.[6]

Despite their differences, the studies reviewed agree on three points. First, natives (including immigrants who have entered the country prior to 1970) contribute more revenues per capita than post-1970 immigrants. This higher contribution results from higher estimated incomes among the native-born than among immigrants. Second, Huddle and Passel agree that legal immigrants contribute more in revenues than amnestied and illegal immigrants, again principally because the estimated incomes of the first are higher. Finally, they

---

[5]There are also some differences among the studies in estimates of per-service costs, but these variations are not large, with one exception. CIS estimated a Social Security payment of $704 per immigrant compared with $66 estimated by Passel. This difference stems from a conceptual disagreement on how to account for Social Security payments—on an actual basis in the year of the study or on a "proportional" basis. We discuss this issue further in the next chapter.

[6]These are approximate estimates made by the authors of this study.

also agree that illegal immigrants cost more in services than they contribute in public revenues, although the size of the "deficits" they estimate differs significantly.

COMPARISON OF STATE AND LOCAL FINDINGS

We reviewed two studies of the costs of immigration to states (Romero, Chang, and Parker, 1994; King, 1994) and four studies of the costs to counties or localities (ISD, 1992; Clark and Passel, 1993; Parker and Rea, 1993; and King, 1994). In contrast to studies of costs at the national level, these studies cover a more comprehensive list of services, including most, if not all, state and local costs of providing public services. Typically, they begin by identifying the total state or county outlays funded from general and special fund revenues, excluding federal transfers to the state level and federal and state transfers to the local level. They then allocate a portion of those outlays to immigrants using varying estimating approaches.

On the revenue side, these studies, like those dealing with the national level, do not include all general and special funds revenues. State-level revenues include a maximum of 80 percent of total general and special fund revenues and typically omit taxes paid by corporations, railroads, public utilities, and insurance companies, as well as fees, licenses, tolls, and fines that may be levied by various state departments. Local-level revenues represent as little as 30 percent of general revenues. Typically excluded are taxes from commercial property (about a third of total property taxes), special assessments (e.g., for fire protection or refuse collection), fees (e.g., for use of parks), fines (e.g., for parking or other violations), interest earnings, and sales of property. Implicitly, these studies assume that immigrants do not contribute to these public revenues.

Table 3 displays the per-capita cost and revenue estimates of these various studies for immigrants as a whole and for subgroups of immigrants, including illegal immigrants. Comparison among these findings should be made carefully because they group immigrants in different ways and because they vary in the relative proportion of service costs and public revenues included. Where groupings of immigrants are similar, the estimates display large differences. Among illegal immigrants, ISD estimated per-capita yearly cost to Los Angeles County of $440 compared with $1,254 in the San Diego

Table 3
State and Local Studies of Costs of Immigration: Per-Capita Public Annual Costs and Revenues by Immigration Status

| | Local Studies | | | | | | | | | State Studies | | | | | | | | |
| | Los Angeles County[a] ISD, 1992 | | | Los Angeles County Clark and Passel, 1993 | | | San Diego County, Parker and Rea, 1993 | | | New Jersey, Local King, 1994 | | | New Jersey State, King, 1994 | | | State of California Romero, Chang, and Parker, 1994 | | |
Immigration Status	Cost	Revenue	Ratio	Cost	Revenue	Ratio	Cost	Revenue	Ratio	Cost	Revenue	Ratio	Cost	Revenue	Ratio	Cost	Revenue	Ratio
Immigrants																		
Illegal	440	38[b]	11.6				1,254	271	4.6							1,990	429	4.6
Citizen children of illegals	366						127[c]									521		
Amnestied	269	65	4.1															
Legal 1980–1992	344	88	3.9															
All above	353[d]	60[d]	5.8	353[d]	123[d]	2.9				602[e]	408[e]	1.5	633[e]	329[e]	1.9			
Native-born	328	182	1.8	328	181	1.8				595	470	1.3	647	343	1.9			
Percentage of total service costs or revenues included in study[f]	100	30		100	30		100			100			100	<75		100	77	

SOURCE: See list of references for full citations of studies.

NOTE: A blank means the information is not available or not applicable.

[a] Excludes school expenditures because they are covered by a special district.

[b] Includes citizen children of illegal immigrants.

[c] Cost of AFDC to citizen children of illegal immigrants.

[d] Includes all who entered after 1980, including amnestied and undocumented immigrants.

[e] Includes all foreign-born immigrants aged 65 or under.

[f] Our approximations.

County study.[7] The latter study's inclusion of costs for some state-provided services—e.g., health, criminal justice, welfare—explains most of this difference. Both studies estimate a fiscal "deficit" for illegal immigrants, but the estimate for L.A. County is 2.5 times greater.

Similarly, large differences are apparent on the revenue side. Clark and Passel, for example, estimate yearly revenues per capita ($123) that are twice as high as those made by ISD ($60)—a difference that is attributable mainly to different estimates of immigrant incomes (Table 3).

These large differences in estimated aggregate costs and revenues mask even greater disparities in estimates for individual services and revenue sources. For instance, Romero, Chang, and Parker (1994) estimated the State of California spent $224 per illegal immigrant for annual Medicaid emergency services compared with San Diego's estimate of $84 (see Table A.3 in the appendix). On the revenue side, the San Diego study assumes that property owners pay the entire property tax while immigrants pay none. Other studies make different assumptions (see Table A.4 in the appendix).

In spite of such differences, the state and local studies generally agree on two points. First, they estimate that neither native-borns nor immigrants pay their way at the state and local levels. This is not surprising since those studies include a full list of outlays but only a partial list of revenues excluding, for instance, transfer payments from higher levels of government. State and local governments have to balance their budgets on an annual basis and generally do. Hence, finding a "deficit" for all residents of a jurisdiction is simply an "accounting" artifact.

Second, where estimates are made separately for immigrants and the native-born, the studies agree that the "deficit" for immigrants is larger than the "deficit" for native-borns. *This finding, however,*

---

[7]Differences in costs per capita may also be caused by differences in levels of services provided across jurisdictions. Such variations, however, are minimized when comparing local jurisdictions within the same state. Also, differences in public outlays would also be reflected in differences in public revenues raised to finance those outlays, also minimizing their effects on net fiscal costs (or benefits).

merely reflects the higher average income, and hence revenues, esti-mated for native-borns.

CONCLUSIONS

Few firm conclusions can be drawn from these studies, given their differences in counts of immigrants, grouping of immigrants (with the exception of illegals) and attribution of service costs or revenues to immigrants. The studies also differ in the range of services and revenues and in the assumptions they make regarding immigrants' incomes, use of services, and incidence of tax payments. In brief, these studies' findings are neither comparable nor comprehensive and do not provide reliable estimates of the net fiscal costs or bene-fits of immigration.

Inconsistencies in coverage and accounting across studies are less likely to affect relative estimates of costs and revenues across sub-groups of immigrants and the native-borns within a given study. In this regard, the studies are generally consistent in finding that illegals contribute less in revenues than amnestied, legals, and native-borns, in that order. Because costs per capita are estimated to be nearly the same across these subgroups, this finding reflects differences in average income across those subgroups rather than in immigration status.

Chapter Three

TOWARD A UNIFORM ACCOUNTING FRAMEWORK

An accurate accounting of the net public costs of immigrants requires reliable information on a large number of parameters:

- The number of immigrants, their immigration status, and appropriate socioeconomic characteristics.

- The *actual* use, for the period of time considered, of all relevant public services provided to immigrants for every family member, by their immigration status.

- The *actual* public costs of providing the relevant services, including both operational and capital costs, and the costs of borrowing funds in cases of deficit financing.

- *Actual* payroll deductions, income and sales tax payments, property tax payments, excise tax payments, fees and other forms of revenue raised from each immigrant (or family of immigrants, as appropriate) by immigration status for the period considered.

Such information is not currently available. Hence, the studies have used various accounting techniques, proxy variables, and assumptions to estimate service use, costs, and revenues.

We have already pointed out that accounting differences among studies have caused significant disparities in their results. When the press and the politicians treat every new study as accurate and definitive, it only adds to the confusion among the public about whom and what to believe. To alleviate this problem, consensus is needed on the appropriate approach to these accounting issues. Consensus must also be developed on a set of rules for uniformly treating key conceptual questions that the studies have failed to address explicity.

This chapter outlines the main issues that need to be addressed to develop such a consensus. Our discussion is organized into three categories:

- Conceptual and accounting issues
- Behavioral assumptions and data availability
- Cost allocation issues.

To amplify these points, we use examples from the studies reviewed.

CONCEPTUAL AND ACCOUNTING ISSUES

To develop a consistent "accounting framework," the following four questions must be addressed: (1) Who is an "immigrant," and what subgroups of immigrants should be distinguished? (2) Which public services ought to be included? (3) Which public revenues ought to be included? and (4) What is the accounting time period?

Defining and Grouping Immigrants

How to define and categorize immigrants and natives are important policy as well as analytical decisions. How an "immigrant" is defined not only affects the count of immigrants but also which costs and revenues are attributed to immigrants, and hence the outcome of the study. Definitions and categories also reflect different policy concerns.

Defining "Immigrant." There is general agreement that all *foreign-born noncitizens* should be defined as "immigrants."[1] There is less agreement about how to treat the U.S.-born children of immigrants and the foreign-born who are naturalized citizens.

---

[1]Even this cannot be taken for granted. As noted earlier, all the studies reviewed in this report excluded immigrants who had entered the country prior to 1970.

The studies reviewed have uniformly excluded the costs of providing public services to the citizen children of legal immigrants. However, these studies differ in their treatment of the costs of providing public services to the citizen children of illegal immigrants—some have excluded them, while others have included them in the "costs of immigrants" column.

Although the choice between these two alternatives is not clear-cut, it will affect cost analyses significantly. One study (Romero, Chang, and Parker, 1994) estimated that attributing the costs of servicing citizen children to their illegal immigrant parents added in excess of 25 percent to the public service costs of illegal immigration (see Table 3).

The argument for excluding citizen children of immigrants from the definition of "immigrants" is a legal/constitutional one: Children born on U.S. soil are guaranteed citizenship by the U.S. Constitution and are citizens by definition. They are entitled to the same services available to other citizens, and hence should be treated as "native-born." But if this argument holds for citizen children, it should also hold for the foreign-born who become naturalized citizens. Consistency then would seem to require that the approximately 30 percent of immigrants who have become naturalized citizens should be excluded from the "immigrant" category.

The argument for including citizen children of immigrants in the definition of "immigrants" is a pragmatic one: If their parents had not immigrated, these citizen children would not have been born here and the public costs of providing services to them would not have been incurred. Hence, their costs should be included with those of their immigrant parents.

Regardless of the choice that is made, it should be applied consistently. We see no rationale for including the costs of citizen children with those of their illegal parents while excluding those costs for citizen children of other immigrants (or for naturalized citizens) as some studies have done (e.g., Huddle, 1993; CIS, 1994). In future studies, the costs of citizen children should be treated uniformly for all immigrant groups. To accommodate both views, these costs could be counted and displayed separately from the costs of their immigrant parents; in any event, they should not be included in the costs attributed to all other native-borns.

Appropriate Unit of Analysis. The treatment of the citizen children of immigrants also has implications for defining the appropriate unit of analysis—an issue overlooked by all the studies reviewed. They all allocated the costs to *individual* immigrants, but accounted for public revenues at the *family* level. An accounting inconsistency arises if the costs of servicing some members of the family are excluded from the "cost" column at the same time that revenues from these members are included from the "revenue" column. The result is an overestimate of the "tax revenues" collected to cover the estimated costs.

There is a similar problem associated with appropriately defining the "immigrant" family—how to treat the many family units that have a mix of adult "immigrants" and "native-born" adults. In the studies reviewed, if the family head is "foreign-born," the family is labeled "immigrant," and all revenues are accounted against the costs attributed to the immigrant head of family, leading to an underestimate of net costs. Arguably, mixed families classified as "immigrant" might be canceled out by those classified as "native-born"—but that is an empirical question to which we do not yet know the answer.

Grouping Immigrants and Native-Borns. Most recent studies have singled out undocumented immigrants as a separate group, reflecting the current concern with illegal immigration. The studies differ, however, in how they have categorized other immigrants. Some distinguish immigrants who are beneficiaries of a specific federal policy (i.e., immigrants amnestied under the Immigration Reform and Control Act of 1986—IRCA), or according to date of entry (i.e., immigrants who have entered since 1970 or 1980). Others simply group all immigrants together regardless of status and date of entry. Authors of these studies have agreed on only one thing: to group native-borns into one category.

There is nothing compelling about these categories. Other justifiable categorizations may be devised, based on such parameters as

- Current criteria for permanent entry (i.e., humanitarian, family, or employment-related).

- Expected level of use of public services.

- Factors expected to affect lifetime contributions to public revenues (e.g., skills and education level, ability to speak English at entry).

Different categorizations imply different policy concerns. Distinctions based on legal status, date of entry, or eligibility for public services reflect the current policy focus on undocumented immigration and attempts by state and local governments to obtain federal funding to compensate them for bearing what they believe is a disproportionate share of the costs of providing services to immigrants. But these are not the only issues that might be addressed. If, for example, a study's goal is to identify policy choices that would maximize contributions to revenues, then the focus should be on those characteristics that differentiate immigrants in terms of their income. Alternatively, if the purpose is to determine how well the current criteria for legal entry meet the objective of minimizing the net fiscal costs of immigration, then distinctions should be drawn among immigrants in terms of how they qualified for entry (e.g., as refugees, for family reunification, or as economic immigrants). The way a study distinguishes among immigrants directly determines the conclusions it will eventually reach. We return to this issue in Chapter Four.

Services to Be Included

Deciding which services and revenues to include in studies of the fiscal costs (benefits) of immigration is perhaps the most critical issue affecting the findings. Decisions made in this regard can mean the difference between showing a net fiscal surplus or a net fiscal deficit for any subgroup of immigrants or native-borns, as was shown in the previous subsection.

Studies of the *national* costs of providing services to immigrants have typically focused on services that are provided *directly* to individuals, services such as education and social services; on some county and local costs; on transfer payments—although there are disagreements on how to account for "social insurance programs," and on grants-in-aid to state and local governments, which constitute about half of federal expenditures (see Table 4). Excluded are large federal budget items such as national defense, research and de-

Table 4

Federal Expenditures by Major Category of Expenditures, 1992

Category of Expenditure	Dollars (billions)	Percent
Purchase	448.8	30.8
National defense	313.8	21.5
Nondefense	135.0	9.2
Transfer payments (net)	624.5	42.8
To persons	608.2	41.7
To rest of world	16.3	1.1
Grant-in-aid to state and local government	171.4	11.7
Net interest	187.1	12.8
Interest paid	219.9	14.7
Less interest received	(32.8)	(2.2)
Subsidies less current surpluses of government enterprises	27.5	1.9
Subsidies	31.7	2.2
Surplus of government enterprises	(4.1)	(.3)
Total	1,459.3	100.0

SOURCE: *Survey of Current Business*, June 1994, Vol. 74, No. 6, Table 3.2.

velopment, general governmental and administrative functions provided by legislative bodies and executive agencies (e.g., the Immigration and Naturalization Service), and interest paid on the national debt.

In contrast to the national-level studies, state and local studies have typically included all the costs accruing to that level of government, including the costs of general government functions. Hence, the treatment of general government functions across studies is inconsistent.[2]

---

[2]Clearly, this issue arises only in comparisons across studies. It does not arise within the context of one study comparing relative costs and revenues among different population subgroups so long as the same services and revenues are included for each population subgroup, as is the case in all studies reviewed here. It may, however, affect the completeness of the study's findings.

Treatment of Indivisible Goods and General Government Functions. Excluding large components of federal expenditures and general government functions (e.g., national defense, research and development, debt payments, highway construction and maintenance) significantly reduces the public costs attributed to immigrants and can be justified on only one of two grounds: either (1) immigrants are deemed not to receive any benefits from those services; or (2) the services—public goods that benefit everyone, such as national defense and roadways—would be provided in the same quantity and quality in the absence of any immigration, so that the marginal cost of providing these services to immigrants is nil.

Both rationales for exclusion are questionable. There is no foundation to support the "no benefit" argument. Immigrants do benefit from a democratic form of governance and from the general infrastructure and other support services conducive to a stable political environment and to economic growth.

The "zero marginal cost" argument is more difficult to dismiss; it has merit from a purely economic accounting point of view. The difficulty with it, however, is determining when and for whom it applies. The same argument could be applied across generations of the native-born as well as to the citizen children of immigrants (see earlier discussion). But as a nation, we have opted to make everyone pay (albeit according to a progressive tax schedule) for general government functions and for indivisible goods, both for equity reasons and because everyone benefits to some extent from such goods and services. Excluding immigrants from "paying" for these services would be akin to arguing that native-borns, including low-income native-borns, should be "subsidizing" immigrants for such services.

If one accepts, as we do, that immigrants ought to pay for general government functions and public goods, it is necessary to decide what portion of the costs for such services should be attributed to immigrants? We come back to this question in the section on "cost allocation issues."

Treatment of Social Insurance Programs. Other programs that present special conceptual difficulties are social insurance programs (e.g., Social Security, Medicare, unemployment insurance, and workers' compensation). Experts disagree on how to treat them, and hence different studies have dealt with them in different ways. These programs raise two interrelated questions to which there is no uniquely "right" answer.

The first question is whether to include social insurance programs at all in computing the fiscal costs of immigration. Arguably, these programs provide pension, job insurance, or health insurance benefits that are primarily self-funded, even though revenues collected for some of these programs may be mixed with general-fund revenues. To the extent that such a program is truly self-funded, this argument speaks for its exclusion.[3] In this event, payroll taxes (or other revenues) used to pay for it should also be excluded from the revenue side.

Most social insurance programs, however, have a redistributive function with some groups of payers receiving more in benefits than they contribute in revenues and vice versa.[4] Moreover, the funds raised from payroll taxes for these programs are treated as general funds and drawn upon on an ongoing basis. Hence, these programs should be included in costs of immigration studies. But—and this is the second question—how should these costs be assessed?

To date, two sharply differing approaches have been used. One approach, used for Social Security (the largest of these programs), has been to attribute to immigrants the estimated value of payments actually made to them during the time period considered by the study (usually a fiscal year). Since most immigrants are not yet of retirement age, the benefits so estimated are currently quite low. The rationale for this approach is that the children of immigrants will eventually pay for the retirement of their parents. Call it the "intergenerational" accounting approach.

Another approach has been to distribute the total payments to foreign-borns proportionally, based on the ratio of the number of im-

---

[3]By "truly," we mean that no general funds are used to cover a "deficit" between revenues and expenditures in these programs for any of the subgroups considered by a study.

[4]The redistributional characteristics of social insurance programs are complex, particularly where pension programs are concerned, because they depend not only on lifetime income, but also on longevity after retirement.

migrants in a given category to the total number of immigrants. Because recent studies have focused on immigrants who have arrived most recently, this method attributes a higher "cost" to immigrants than the first. For instance, CIS, which used the latter method, estimated Social Security costs "incurred" by post-1970 immigrants to be ten times higher ($704) than Passel, which used the first method ($66) (see Table A.3 in the appendix). In this latter view, new immigrants are "held liable" for supporting the pensions of previous waves of immigrants. Call it the "intra-immigrant" accounting approach.

Whether one should adopt one of these or any other approach is not just a technical question. It depends on one's view of who should be paying for whom when there is a large time lag between making contributions and receiving benefits. Considering that contributions to a pension/retirement program are payments for benefits received later, a lifetime actuarial method (see below) to estimate the costs of social insurance programs should be preferred.

Ongoing Versus Lifetime Costs

The preceding discussion raises an even broader question: Should we measure costs and contributions at a particular point in time (the "ongoing" approach) or over the lifetime of an individual (the "lifetime" approach)? When there is a large inflow of young immigrants in a short period of time, as there is now, they may make less use of services initially than they will at a later time in their lives, particularly after they leave the labor force. In the meantime, they contribute taxes to the general revenues. The "ongoing" approach to cost accounting is the appropriate one if the primary policy goal is to balance the budget on an annual basis. But if the goal is to understand the costs/contributions made by an individual over time, the "lifetime" approach to assessing costs of immigration is the appropriate one.

Neither approach is inherently right or wrong. Each provides a different piece of information and answers a different set of questions that are especially complex, particularly for social insurance programs (see above) and services that have an investment component—that is, where an initial expenditure of resources is expected to have a long-term payoff. A classic case of such an investment is education, which involves a large investment in the early life of an indi-vidual and large returns in the form of higher earnings, and hence, higher public revenues much later in life. Health care services may also involve large trade-offs over time: higher costs in a given year for preventive health care in exchange for lower costs later for catas-trophic illnesses or other social costs.

Revenues to Be Included

Just as the studies reviewed did not include all the public services from which immigrants derive benefits, neither do they include all revenues accruing to the public treasury. Typically, the studies have been more comprehensive on the revenue side at the national levels, and more comprehensive on the costs side at the state and local lev-els, introducing a bias in the estimates of net fiscal surpluses or deficits.

Five major types of revenues have been excluded or otherwise treated unevenly across studies:

- Bank, corporation, and insurance taxes
- Commercial property taxes
- Interest earnings
- Fines, fees, special assessments, and special funds taxes
- Utility revenues.

The *bank, corporation, and insurance tax* category is the largest revenue type that is omitted at both the federal and the state levels (see Table 5). Omission of these revenues is all the more problematic because the costs of providing public services to businesses and banks are typically not deducted from the costs allocated to individual residents thus inflating costs and deflating revenues attributed to immigrants. Either the costs of services to businesses should be excluded from the costs attributed to immigrants, or a portion of these revenues should be deemed to be contributed by immigrants.

Commercial property taxes also raise sizable revenues for counties. For instance, they contribute 37 percent of the total property taxes

Table 5

Annual Public Revenues by Level of Government and by Source, 1992[a]

Sources of Revenues	Federal		State and Local Governments		State of California		Los Angeles County[a]	
	Dollars (Billions)	Percent	Dollars (Billions)	Percent	Dollars (Billions)	Percent	Dollars (Billions)	Percent
Personal tax and nontax receipts	490.8	41.5	154.0	18.4	17.7	21.7		
Income taxes	478.0		116.7		17.2			
Estate and gift taxes	11.3				.5			
Nontaxes	1.4		18.3					
Other			19.0					
Corporate profits tax accruals	120.2	10.2	26.0	3.1	5.7	7.0		
Indirect business tax and nontax accruals	81.3	6.9	421.5	50.3	31.1	38.3	3.5	37.2
Sales tax			200.8		20.8		.1	
Excise tax	46.8				.3		.03	
Property tax			177.7				2.2[b]	
Custom duties	18.3							
Nontaxes	16.2							
Other[c]			43.0		10.1		1.2	

Table 5—continued

Sources of Revenues	Federal		State and Local Governments		State of California		Los Angeles County[a]	
	Dollars (Billions)	Percent	Dollars (Billions)	Percent	Dollars (Billions)	Percent	Dollars (Billions)	Percent
Contributions for social insurance	490.7	41.5	64.9	7.7			1.0	10.6
Grants-in-aid from other levels of government			171.4	20.4	26.7	32.9	4.9	52.1
Total	1,183.0	100.0	837.8	100.0	81.2	100.0	9.4	100.0

SOURCES: *Survey of Current Business*, June 1994, Vol. 74, No. 6, Tables 3.2 and 3.3; California State Budget; and U.S. Bureau of Census, Census for Los Angeles County.

NOTE: Individual items may not add to totals because of rounding. A blank means not relevant.

[a]Figures for Los Angeles County are for the year 1989–1990.

[b]Residential properties contribute 63 percent to total property tax revenues, and commercial properties, 37 percent.

[c]Includes mix of fines, fees, special assessments, and special funds revenues.

levied by the County of Los Angeles. However, the costs of providing local services to businesses have typically not been deducted from the overall costs allocated to immigrants, leading to the same bias mentioned above.

We noted earlier that *interests* on general debt are not always included in the "costs of services." Similarly, interest earnings from investment funds or overnight tax revenue investments are not accounted on the revenue side. The issue would be of lesser import if the two were generally in balance, but they rarely are. The federal government has consistently run a fiscal deficit in recent times. At the local level, however, the reverse has often been true. For instance, the County of Los Angeles earned more interest than it paid in debt service in 1990: $309 versus $240 million.

Fines, fees, special assessments, and special funds revenues constitute a significant portion of the revenues collected by federal, state, and local governments. For instance, they constitute 18 percent of California state general and special revenues and 35 percent of general revenues of the County of Los Angeles. The studies we have reviewed generally have included the major special funds: motor vehicle fees, tobacco and liquor taxes, and horse racing taxes. Generally excluded, however, are smaller special funds revenues such as regulatory licenses and permits, penalties on traffic violations, rentals on state property, state and local beach and park service fees, oil and gas revenues, and other miscellaneous items.

Utility revenues are generally small, but can vary significantly across jurisdictions.

These two last categories of revenues raise two additional issues. The first is a consistency issue. If any of these revenues are used to defray the costs of services included on the costs side, then they should be included on the revenue side. Studies appear to have been inconsistent in implementing this basic principle of accounting. The second issue concerns special funds or user fees that are earmarked for a specific purpose. To the extent that no general funds are used to cover a portion of the costs of that service, they arguably can be excluded. Another approach, supported by research findings, is that earmarked public funds are a substitute, though imperfect, for general funds, and, hence, all public funds, including categorical funds, should be treated as general funds.

BEHAVIORAL ASSUMPTIONS AND DATA AVAILABILITY

Until such time as adequate resources are available for collecting the necessary data on the services used and the revenues contributed by immigrants, studies of the costs of immigration will continue to rely on proxy information. As a result, we must be prepared to accept broad variations in estimates regardless of whether agreement can be reached on uniform treatment of the conceptual questions discussed in the preceding subsection. Below, we outline the main problems with the use of such proxy information and illustrate how the use of different proxies can lead to significant variations in findings.

Estimating Use of Public Services

In lieu of direct measures of service utilization by immigrants, the assumption most commonly made by the studies reviewed is that immigrants use services in proportion to their numbers, and no adjustments are made to account for variations in intensity of use over the period of time considered. Direct census and administrative data on actual service usage have been used in only a few instances, including primary and secondary education, occasionally criminal justice, and emergency medical assistance (Medicaid). But even in these instances, assumptions had to be made that significantly shaped the results.

In the case of education, a key factor affecting the estimated costs is the estimate of the number of undocumented children who are of school age and actually attend public schools. The difficulty of making reliable estimates of this number is illustrated by the fact that estimates of the number of illegal immigrant children in California's schools differ by 20 percent or more depending on the study (Romero, Chang, and Parker, 1994, and Clark et al., 1994).

In the case of health care, the estimates are based on surveys on amnestied immigrants' use of health services, which form the basis to claim federal reimbursement under IRCA's State Legalization

Impact Assistance Grants (SLIAG). Alternatively, estimates of the use of emergency services covered under the federal Omnibus Budget and Reconciliation Act of 1986 (OBRA) have also been used. In both instances, only a portion of total public health costs—primarily emergency and prenatal care—were included.

A 1991 RAND pilot survey of Salvadoran and Filipino immigrants residing in Los Angeles allowed us to assess the extent to which the "proportionality rule" used to allocate the costs of most other services may be biasing the results. These data were also used to test the common assumption that utilization of specific services does not vary with immigration status or income.[5] The data raise serious questions about the validity of these assumptions.

The survey asked respondents whether they or anyone in their family had used a broad array of public and private services at least once over the past 12 months. Table 6 shows the results for four types of services: income transfer and nutrition programs, health services, health insurance coverage, and other services (e.g., education, libraries, and public transport).

The following observations affecting the estimates of costs of immigration can be made from our survey results:

- Undocumented immigrants are more likely than their legal counterparts to use public hospitals and clinics and less likely to be members of health maintenance organizations (HMOs). A potential reason for this pattern may be found in the pattern of public versus private insurance coverage: Undocumented immigrants are less likely to be covered by private insurance or an HMO.

- Although undocumented immigrants themselves are not eligible for AFDC or food stamps, they benefit indirectly from these programs either through their eligible children or relatives, so perhaps a portion of these costs should be attributed to undocumented immigrants.

---

[5]For a detailed description of this survey and its findings see DaVanzo et al., 1994. The survey interviewed 382 Salvadoran and 273 Filipino immigrants in selected communities of Los Angeles.

Table 6

Use of Services by Immigration Status and by Type of Program: Salvadoran and Filipino Immigrants, 1991

Type of Program	Salvadoran Immigrants					Filipino Immigrants			
	Undocu-mented	TPS[a]	Temporary Visa	Permanent Resident	All	Permanent Resident	Citizen	All
Transfer Programs (percent)								
AFDC	14	10	13	6	9	2	1	1
Food stamps	22	17	18	14	17	4	1	2
Women, Infants and Children (supplemental food program, Department of Agriculture)	33	28	34	20	26	6	0	2
Unemployment compensation	8	8	8	10	9	13	8	10
Workers' compensation	4	6	0	8	6	3	3	3
Health Services (services)								
Public hospital	30	24	29	21	25	10	10	10
County, free, or family clinics	52	50	53	35	45	16	10	12
Prenatal clinics	17	20	16	14	16	6	4	4
Private doctor or clinic	31	48	39	51	45	52	62	58

Table 6—continued

Type of Program	Salvadoran Immigrants					Filipino Immigrants		
	Undocu-mented	TPS[a]	Temporary Visa	Permanent Resident	All	Permanent Resident	Citizen	All
Health Insurance								
Coverage (percent)								
Any health insurance	39	40	37	44	41	87	90	88
Government program	35	28	32	22	28	26	26	26
Private insurance	3	7	11	15	10	56	58	57
HMO	7	10	3	18	12	40	53	49
Other Services (percent)								
School attended								
Public	100	100	100	93	95	85	76	78
Private or parochial	0	0	0	7	5	15	24	22
Public transport	70	61	66	60	63	25	28	26
Recreation	52	46	37	58	52	62	71	66
Libraries	21	22	32	32	28	47	71	62
Average annual income (dollars)	10,250	10,800	11,250	13,000	11,485	37,630	50,000	47,325
N	92	89	38	161	380	89	176	265

SOURCE: DaVanzo et al., (1994), Tables 5.5–5.9, pp. 46–49.

[a]Temporary Protective Status.

- The extent to which children attend public or private school appears to depend both on income and immigration status. The children of the low-income Salvadoran immigrants attend public school exclusively. The only exception is for a small percentage of children (7 percent) of Salvadoran permanent residents. In contrast, from one out of six to one out of four school-age children of Filipino immigrants attend private or parochial school.

DaVanzo et al. (1994) assessed the extent to which immigration status, family income, and other factors might affect use of services. The results of their multivariate analysis suggest that the use of public services is generally not affected by immigration status, including undocumented status. The main factors affecting the use of transfer programs and health services are income and number of children, most particularly children aged five or under. In addition, the use of special purpose services (libraries, public transport, parks, and recreation) is affected by factors influencing the need for the service in the first place, such as income, number of children, English proficiency, or desire to change immigration status. In brief, the RAND results do not support the "proportionality" assumption for service utilization across immigrant groups. There is no reason to believe that it would hold across native groups either.

Estimating Public Revenues

In lieu of direct measures of the public revenues collected from immigrants, estimates of revenues collected are made by first estimating (i.e., making assumptions about) a number of factors, including (1) individual earnings, (2) family incomes, (3) portion of income earned in the United States that is spent abroad, (4) incidence of actual payroll deductions and actual tax filings, (5) consumption of items subject to taxation, (6) tax rates applicable to individuals or groupings of "similar" individuals, and (7) the actual revenue sources—individuals, families, or businesses.

Of these seven factors, only individual earnings and family income are fairly accurately measured for foreign-borns by the decennial censuses or by the annual Current Population Survey (CPS). A major problem with census or CPS data is that they do not provide information on immigration status; hence, assumptions must be made about the earnings and income profile of immigrants with different immigration statuses. Assumptions made regarding the other factors needed to estimate public revenues from immigrants have also varied significantly across studies. Those with the largest effect on findings are discussed below.

Assumptions Regarding Remittances. Some studies assume that immigrants spend all of their income in this country, while others estimate that a portion of that income is sent home in the form of remittances. Estimates of remittances vary from 6 to 12 percent across studies (King, 1994; ISD, 1992). Of course, the relative value of remittances can be expected to vary between immigrants of different immigration status, length of stay in the country, and income. These variations are typically ignored. Indeed, we have encountered just such variations in our survey of immigrants from El Salvador and the Philippines. Table 7 suggests that the proportion of families sending remittances, as well as the amount of these remittances, is similar across income groups, and ranges from $900 to $1,400 annually per family. As a percentage of income, however, remittances vary from a low of 2 percent to a high of 13 percent, being much higher for the poorer Salvadorans than the better-off Filipinos.

Incidence of Actual Payroll Deductions and Actual Tax Filings. Estimates of the incidence of actual payroll deductions and federal and state tax filings vary significantly across studies. Some assume high rates of compliance, while others accept the findings of one study that measured a 56 percent compliance for payroll tax payments among undocumented immigrants and an 83 percent compliance among legal immigrants (North and Houston, 1976).

The 1991 RAND survey of Salvadoran and Filipino immigrants suggests that payroll tax deductions and federal income tax filing are highly dependent on immigration status (Table 8). About half of the illegal immigrants working at the time of the interview had payroll taxes deducted and less than 40 percent had filed a federal or state tax return. Permanent immigrants reported the highest incidence of payroll tax deductions and income tax filings. But even among those with the same immigration status, there are variations among immigrants. Salvadoran permanent residents were less likely than Filipino permanent residents to have their payroll taxes deducted or

Table 7

Average Remittance and Income by Immigration Status: Salvadoran and Filipino Immigrants, 1991

Remittance/ Income	Salvadoran Immigrants					Filipino Immigrants		
	Undocumented	TPS[a]	Temporary Visa	Permanent Resident	All	Permanent Resident	Citizen	All
Percentage of families sending remittances	73	82	92	72	77	69	75	72
Average income ($)	10,250	10,800	11,250	13,000	11,567	37,630	50,000	42,083
Average annual remittance ($)	946	1,311	1,493	1,039	1,132	910	1,330	1,197
Remittance as percentage of income	9.2	12.1	13.3	8.0	9.8	2.4	2.7	2.8

SOURCE: 1991 RAND survey of Salvadoran and Filipino immigrants in Los Angeles.

[a]Temporary Protective Status.

Table 8

Federal Tax Filings and Payroll Deductions by Immigration Status: Salvadoran and Filipino Immigrants, 1991

Tax Filings and Payroll Deductions	Salvadoran Immigrants					Filipino Immigrants		
	Undocumented	TPS[a]	Temporary Visa	Permanent Resident	All	Permanent Resident	Citizen	All
Filed federal taxes[b] (percent)	38	54	63	84	64	91	95	93
Payroll deductions[c] (percent)								
Any	50	52	53	72	60	97	96	97
Federal taxes	46	51	37	72	57	94	96	95
State taxes	50	49	40	72	57	94	96	95
Social Security	46	51	44	70	57	91	91	91
Health insurance	9	6	12	25	15	47	62	52
Average annual income (dollars)	10,250	10,800	11,250	13,000	11,567	37,630	50,000	47,325

SOURCE: DaVanzo et al., 1994, p. 51.

[a]Temporary Protective Status.

[b]Percentage of all respondents.

[c]Percentage of respondents who worked the week preceding the interview.

to file federal tax returns, reflecting significant differences in occupational structure and incomes.[6]

Although our findings are based on a relatively small sample and cannot be generalized to all immigrants, they support the hypothesis that the incidence of public revenues varies by immigration status, independently from income.

COST ALLOCATION ISSUES

The preceding discussion raises a number of critical cost allocation questions that have either been ignored or implicitly minimized in the studies we have reviewed. The most important of these are discussed below.

Costs to Individuals Versus Costs to Households

A number of federal, state, and local entitlement benefits and services are provided directly to individuals (e.g., cash payments, Social Security, schooling, nutrition programs, and training programs). However, even in such cases, allocation of the full value of the payments or full cost of the service to the eligible recipient is not without ambiguity. Other individuals may directly or indirectly benefit from the payment or provision of the service. Such is true, for instance, of the illegal parents of citizen children eligible for AFDC payments, as noted earlier. And such is the case with nutrition programs, which are preventive in nature, and which indirectly serve general public health interests and might even save on future remedial or rehabilitation services.

In cases such as those cited above, the question arises whether the value of the benefits accruing to others should be deducted from costs assigned to the individual immigrant recipients. The answer to this question will depend on one's view of immigration. If one believes that the service would not have been provided if the immigrant were not here in the first place, then the full costs ought to be allocated to the immigrant. But if one believes that the immigrant

---

[6]For a detailed discussion of these issues see DaVanzo et al., 1994, pp. 50–53.

would be here even without the service, then only the costs less the benefits to others of the service ought to be allocated to the individual immigrant.

A different issue arises with services that are not directly allocated to individuals, such as fire and police protection, which arguably protect housing units and commercial properties in which families live and conduct business. Should the costs of such services be allocated proportionately to the number of households or to the number of individuals? All the studies reviewed here have used a per-person allocation algorithm.

Costs to Individuals Versus Costs to Businesses

At the same time that the studies reviewed have excluded corporate tax payments from the revenue side, they have prorated the total costs of public services to individuals. For some services, such as fire and police protection, general government functions, and even garbage collection, such an allocation is clearly questionable. Businesses benefit from the provision of those services and hence, a portion of their costs should be allocated to them.

Average Versus Marginal Costs

What cost basis should be used in assigning costs for services that can be provided with minimal, if any, additional operational costs is a critical issue. Fixed costs—such as building and/or maintaining a facility or administering a program—may not vary over a broad range of service recipients. But at some point, substantial incremental costs are required to build new facilities. What approach to adopt in allocating such costs is both a technical and a political decision. A *marginal* cost approach is consistent with a focus on the "cash costs" of providing the service to an increased number of people. In selecting this approach, one should be prepared to attribute to immigrants the entire capital costs of building new facilities should these be necessitated by the population growth they generate. An *average* cost approach—total cost of service divided by total number of recipients—is consistent with a focus on "benefits" of the services, because the immigrants benefit equally with the rest of the population in the provision of the service. These marginal and average cost approaches provide different pieces of information to policymakers. The first measures the costs in additional public funds needed to extend a service to a specified increment of the population. The second measures what everyone ought to be charged for the service, were the burden of paying for the service distributed equitably according to the level of benefit received.

Employees Versus Employers

A final allocation issue arises when revenues are collected in some predetermined proportion from both employees and employers (such as payroll taxes for Social Security, unemployment compensation, and Medicare). This issue has been treated differently by different studies. Passel (1994) and Romero, Chang, and Parker (1994) for instance, deemed that the entire employee and employer components of payroll taxes are revenues "contributed" by the employee. In effect, they assume that the employer portion of Social Security payments is passed through to the employee in the form of lower wages and/or benefits. Parker and Rea (1993) also deemed both the employee and employer portions of the payroll tax to be paid by the employee. However, because payroll tax payments made by employers are deductible for the purpose of computing corporate taxes, they deducted the implied "tax expenditure" amounting to about one-third of the employer payments. They reasoned that the payroll taxes collected are partially offset by the "loss" in corporate taxes. CIS (1994), however, deemed only half of the employer portion of the payroll tax to be revenue "contributed" by the immigrant employee. It relied on econometric findings that only about half of the payroll tax paid by the employer can be deemed to be actually paid by the employee in the form of a lower salary or benefits. The rest is passed on to consumers and/or absorbed by the employer in the form of lower profits (Ehrenberg and Smith, 1991).

Which of the above approaches is the "right" one in computing payroll revenues attributable to any subgroup of individuals in the labor force? Once again, the answer to this question depends on a number of factors. It depends in part upon the extent to which immigrants are substitutes for or complements to native-born workers and the extent to which immigration affects the wages and the incomes of the native-born, either positively or negatively. As noted earlier, the direction and magnitude of these dynamic effects of immigration remain controversial.

Chapter Four

RECASTING THE POLICY DEBATE

The discussion in the previous chapters has demonstrated three key points:

First, prior studies prove little beyond the fact that most recent immigrants have low incomes and families with low incomes contribute less to public revenues than those with high incomes do. In essence, the finding that undocumented immigrants are net consumers of public services is more a product of their low incomes than of their immigration status.

Second, without a consistent accounting framework, the findings of prior studies are not really comparable despite the fact that many seem, at first glance, to share a common heritage.

Third, without both a consistent framework and additional data on service usage and revenue contributions, there is little hope for a definitive answer to the question of how much immigrants actually cost the public treasury at any level of government, whether federal, state, or local.

In sum, while suggesting that recent immigrants have been net consumers of public resources, existing studies do not provide a definitive answer to exactly how great that cost is and how it differs across categories of immigrants. Also, by using an annual cost accounting framework, they limit themselves to addressing a short-term policy issue, such as whether immigrants cost more in a given year than they contribute to the public coffers.

The focus on a particular year's fiscal costs that characterizes the current policy debate has overshadowed the economic, social, and cultural benefits of immigration documented in past studies. This is not surprising, given current economic conditions and increases in immigration flows. A national recession that has been particularly severe and prolonged in the state with the largest concentration of immigrants—California—combined with widespread federal, state, and local government budget shortfalls have focused public attention on the short-term effects that immigration has on the native-borns' standard of living and on state and local governments' ability to maintain public infrastructure and services at historic levels.

These short-term concerns carry over into the long term as well. There is a concern that growing numbers of immigrants with low levels of education are inconsistent with the development of an economy that increasingly demands a more highly educated labor force. Similarly, there are concerns about the country's ability to strike a balance between continuing population growth and environmental "sustainability." In this instance, immigration, a major past and projected future contributor to population growth, is viewed as threatening that balance.

The current fiscal studies have not addressed these longer-term issues; neither have they reached conclusions, that outweigh the findings of other studies that have focused on the broader economic and social effects of immigration. However, studies of the fiscal costs of immigration, appropriately designed and supported by suitable data, have the potential to inform decisions about both longer- and shorter-term issues by contributing useful information to enable policymakers to determine

- Which and how many immigrants should be allowed to enter the country.

- Which public services should be provided to immigrants and at what costs.

- Whether the federal government should reimburse state and local governments for the services they provide to immigrants and, if so, in what amounts.

We elaborate on these points below.

CRITERIA FOR ENTRY AND ELIGIBILITY TO RECEIVE SERVICES

The questions of which immigrants, and how many, should enter the country, and which public services should be extended to them, are interrelated. Policy in the first two areas has traditionally been driven by long-term economic, humanitarian, and social considerations. To explicitly factor in the public costs and benefits of immigrants would represent a real departure from past practice. To date, such costs have played a very minor role in policy, with the exception of their inclusion among the factors used to set annual refugee quotas under the 1980 Refugee Act and under an unevenly enforced provision of disqualifying immigrants who might become a public charge from permanent residence. The use of a fixed set of preference categories and a constant annual immigrant ceiling testifies to the fact that, historically, short-term fiscal cost factors were to be ignored in determining the number and characteristics of legal immigrants and the services they were eligible to receive.

If nothing else, the current policy debate has brought to the fore the issue of whether fiscal costs over the short and/or the long term should become an explicit factor in the nation's immigration and refugee policies. Whether such a policy shift is desirable depends upon the political trade-offs we may be willing to make among potentially competing objectives of immigration and other social policies (e.g., providing asylum to refugees, ensuring equal treatment to residents, promoting family unification).

Determining how to factor in fiscal costs in formulating immigration policy requires taking a long-term as well as a short-term perspective. In essence, we need to know not only whether immigrants in the aggregate consume more than they contribute in any one year but also what services they use and what revenues they contribute over the entire course of their lifetime. We also need to distinguish among immigrants along those dimensions that are most relevant to their long-term economic success and/or use of public services. Neither of these requirements has received any real attention in the studies reviewed.

Identifying the factors that lead to high/low use of public services and economic progress of immigrants over time requires a different analytical approach from that which has been used in current studies. It would require that considerable attention be given to the characteristics of entering individuals and families that will play the most important role in determining their eventual success. Such characteristics would include, at a minimum, the criteria under which they qualified for entry (e.g., family reunification, humanitarian, or employment-related). But they should also include characteristics that might be considered in the future to determine eligibility for permanent entry (e.g., education level, ability to speak English, skills and work experience, and income of family members already in the country).

Similarly, the specific services that immigrants use should be evaluated in much the same way as any investment: Does the investment pay off over the long term, i.e., are the costs of providing the service recovered over the life of the investment? Answers to this question would go a long way toward determining which services provided to immigrants pay off in terms of higher future revenues and which do not. This line of inquiry would provide more reliable and policy-relevant information than the current short-term and undifferentiated approach to estimating the public costs of immigration. In particular, it would help determine whether to change current entry criteria and, if so, in what way. It would also provide information on which groups are high users of state and local services and assist in determining the level of federal assistance needed to cover the costs of those services.

We are not suggesting that consideration of immigrants' effects on the public treasury should necessarily become a factor in determining which immigrants to admit. Indeed, several studies (e.g., Fix and Passel, 1994) indicate, for example, that refugees admitted on humanitarian grounds during the past 20 years, are far and away the highest users of some public services. The federal government has recognized the special needs of refugees, making them eligible for a host of services for which other immigrants are not eligible and assuming the responsibility for financing these services. Clearly, using a fiscal cost-benefit criterion as the basis for admitting refugees would conflict with the humanitarian objectives of U.S. refugee policy. Whether such trade-offs are desirable is essentially a political question, but the eventual implications of those trade-offs should be examined in a longer-term analytical framework, not just in the short term: Who would benefit and who would get hurt? Which immigrants from which countries might be excluded? What would it mean for enforcement? And so on.

FEDERAL TRANSFER PAYMENTS

Whether the federal government ought to reimburse state and local governments for their costs of providing services to immigrants is not a question that can be answered exclusively on analytical grounds. This is an issue that goes to the heart of federal-state relationships and responsibilities and to the question of "unfunded" federal mandates. Elsewhere we have argued that because only the federal government can effectively intervene to control the number of immigrants entering the country, it should bear a greater share of the public costs of providing services to immigrants than it does currently (Vernez, 1993). A precedent for this practice was set in the Immigration Reform and Control Act of 1986, which authorized $1 billion per year for four years to reimburse state governments for the costs of providing public services to immigrants granted amnesty under IRCA. The funds authorized for these State Legalization Assistance Grants were never fully appropriated, due in part to the stringent eligibility verification and financial accounting procedures required for federal reimbursement (Liu, 1991). But in the past few years, the states most affected by immigration—California, Florida, New York, Texas, and Illinois—have again pressed for federal reimbursement, specifically for the costs of services provided to illegal immigrants.

Although several studies have attempted to estimate how much state and local jurisdictions spend on providing such services, our review suggests that none provides a reliable estimate of the magnitude of these costs for the reasons outlined above. The U.S. General Accounting Office (1994) reached a similar conclusion in its more limited review of three studies that attempted to estimate the costs of providing education, health, and correction services to illegal immigrants in California.

A principal argument that state and local governments have made for federal reimbursement is the fact that the federal government collects more tax revenues from immigrants than state and local governments taken together. Senator Barbara Boxer of California articulated this argument when she wrote to President Clinton that "because most revenues from immigrants accrue to the federal government . . . an appropriate use of these revenues would be to reimburse states and localities for uncovered costs."[1]

Table 9 indicates that the federal government does indeed receive about 60 percent of all public revenues collected in taxes and from other sources. But it also spends more providing services—including transfer payments to states and localities—than all other levels of government. The issue, then, is not with the accuracy of the data but rather with the assumption that all revenues collected by the federal government from immigrants should be returned, in their entirety, to reimburse states and localities. (In all of the studies that we reviewed, the estimates of "uncovered" state and local costs exceed the estimates of revenues the federal government has received from illegal immigrants.)

Underlying this assumption are two implicit arguments. The first is that the federal government provides no services to illegal immigrants. This is factually wrong. While the marginal federal costs of

Table 9

Federal and State and Local Government Revenues and Expenditures, 1993

Level of Government	Total Revenues		Expenditures	
	Dollars (Billions)	Percent	Dollars (Billions)	Percent
Federal	1,269.5	59.0	1,495.9	62.8[a]
State and local	881.1	41.0	886.2	37.2
Total	2,150.6	100.0	2,382.1	100.0

SOURCE: U.S. Department of Commerce, *Survey of Current Business*, Vol. 74, No. 6, June 1994, Tables 3.2 and 3.3.

[a] The difference between the $1,495.9 billion federal expenditures and the $1,269.5 billion revenues reflects the federal budget deficit. By the same token, state and local governments exhibited a small surplus.

---

[1] Transmittal letter to the President of the United States dated November 29, 1994; sent with a copy of the U.S. General Accounting Office's *Illegal Aliens: Assessing Estimates of Financial Burden on California*, 1994.

extending coverage of such services as national defense, policymaking, and general government administration may be small, this is not true for all services. The federal government pays at least half the costs of providing emergency health care, nutrition, AFDC, and many other services provided by states and localities to both immigrants and the native-born.

Even if those costs are disregarded, the assumption that the federal government has no claim on revenues collected from undocumented or other immigrants must rest on the assumption that the costs of providing public goods to all residents should be solely born by native-born citizens. This would seem to violate basic equity principles.

RECOMMENDATIONS

Existing studies of the costs of immigration do not provide a reliable or accurate estimate of the net costs and benefits of immigration—even when those costs and benefits are defined narrowly. Moreover, without reaching consensus on a host of conceptual and accounting issues, we doubt that additional studies will shed light on these important policy questions. Consequently, we recommend the following:

First, the research and policy communities need to recognize that the available data are inadequate for making reliable estimates of the fiscal costs of immigration. Instead of conducting more studies with these data, more emphasis should be placed on developing a commonly accepted framework for estimating the costs and on collecting the data required for that framework. In addition, much more attention should be paid a to longer-term perspective on immigration and to considering important policy questions from that perspective.

Clearly, the issue of federal reimbursement for state and local costs of providing services to illegal immigrants is a pressing one that cannot simply be ignored until all the necessary conceptual and data problems have been solved. However, this issue is not amenable to a purely analytical answer. Should a political decision be made in favor of reimbursement, a common accounting framework will be required against which to measure the best range of estimates that currently exist. Such a framework could be developed by some sort of joint federal-state task force.

Second, if federal and state governments are indeed serious about answering the policy questions that are dominating the current immigration policy debate, they will have to provide the resources to support that effort. Such an effort will require agreement on conceptual issues, a common accounting framework, and data collection efforts.[2] It will also require formulating a longer-term framework to consider whether minimizing the public costs of immigration should be an added objective of U.S. immigration and refugee policy. Barring such an investment in building consensus on these conceptual and analytical issues, we are unlikely to make real progress on them.

Finally, current concern about the fiscal costs of immigration should not be allowed to obsure the fact that those costs are only one dimension of a broader set of issues—the economic, social, cultural, and distributional costs and benefits of immigration.

---

[2]Elsewhere (DaVanzo et al., 1994), we have estimated that an effort to collect the necessary information on tax contributions, use of public services, and immigration status would cost about $7 million.

SUPPORTING TABLES

Table A.1

National Studies of Costs of Immigration: Annual Per-Capita Service Costs (Dollars) for Immigrants Who Entered the Country Between 1970 and 1992, 1992

Service	Studies		
	Huddle, 1993	Passel, 1994	CIS, 1994
Education			
K–12	834	684	707
Bilingual education			
Compensatory education	21		22
Adult education			
Student aid	130	104	109
(Public) postsecondary education			
Head Start	2	(a)	(a)
Nutrition, public assistance			
School lunch	19	(b)	(b)
AFDC	144	100	105
Supplemental Security Income	118		109
Food stamps	82	44	46
Nutrition for the elderly	1		
General assistance	14	24	26[c]
Women infants and children (WIC) (supplemented food program)	14	13	14
Health			
Medicaid	441	427	448
Supplemental Medicare			114
Other assistance programs			
Community service and grants	14		15
Unemployment compensation	93		97
Housing assistance	55	48	51
Low-income energy	6		
Job Training and Partnership Act	14	(c)	(c)
Refugee programs	20		
Federal worker benefits			64
Veteran benefits			19
Earned income tax credit			99
Social Security		66	704

Table A.1—continued

Service	Studies Huddle, 1993	Studies Passel, 1994	Studies CIS, 1994
Other costs			
Highway use			242
Corrections	125		248
Interest costs of full form			446
Net county costs	487	212	363
Net city costs			429
Other		441	
Total	2,638	2,156	4,476

SOURCE: See list of references for full citations of studies.

NOTE: A blank means the item is not included. Individual items may not add to totals because of rounding.

[a]Included with estimate for WIC.

[b]Included with estimate for K–12.

[c]Included with estimate for general assistance.

Table A.2

**National Studies of Costs of Immigration: Annual Per-Capita Public
Revenues (Dollars) Contributed by Immigrants Who Entered
the Country Between 1970 and 1992, 1992**

	Studies		
Taxes Included	Huddle, 1993	Passel, 1994	CIS, 1994
Federal taxes			
Income	453	891	935[a]
Excise (alcohol and tobacco)	106	70	73
Federal Insurance Contributions Act (FICA)		1252	984
Unemployment insurance		77	41
Gasoline		55	58[a]
State taxes			
Income	67	162	170
Sales	228	466	488
Excise (alcohol and tobacco)	36	68	72
Gasoline		63	66[a]
Vehicle license and registration		45	47[a]
Lottery	71	66	69[a]
County and local			
Sales	30	119	125[a]
Property	56	310	325[a]
Total	1,051	3,644	3,453

SOURCE: See list of references for full citations of studies.

NOTE: A blank means the item is not included. Individual items may not add to totals because of rounding.

[a]Accepts the estimate by Passel (1994), but applies it to a smaller estimated population.

Table A.3

State and Local Studies of Costs (Dollars) of Immigration: Annual Per-Capita Costs by Type of Service

Type of Service	Studies				
	ISD, 1992[a]	Romero, Chang, and Parker, 1994[b]	Parker and Rea, 1993[b]	King, 1994[c] (State)	King, 1994[c] (Local)
Education					
K–12	400	889	255	212	304
English as a second language			15	4	
Postsecondary					
Nutrition, public assistance					
AFDC			127[d]	15	5
Food stamps					
Pharmacy assistance for the elderly					
General assistance			6[e]		
Children's services	1		8		
Social services	25				
Health					
Medicaid		229[f]	84	17	
Public health	123		137[g]		
Mental health	2		7		
Other assistance programs					
Unemployment compensation			36		

Table A.3—continued

Type of Service		Studies			
	ISD, 1992[a]	Romero, Chang, and Parker, 1994[b]	Parker and Rea, 1993[b]	King, 1994[c] (State)	King, 1994[c] (Local)
Law enforcement/ corrections	153	275[h]	689[i]		
Adult					
Juvenile					
All other	53	596	16[j]	385	293
Total	357[k]	1,989	1,382	633	602

SOURCE: See list of references for full citations of studies.

NOTE: A blank indicates the item was not included. No independent estimate of costs is included because none was made by Clark and Passel, 1993. Individual items may not add to totals because of rounding.

[a]Average figures for illegal, amnestied, or permanent resident immigrants who entered after 1980.

[b]Average figures for illegal immigrants only.

[c]Average figures for all immigrants as of 1980.

[d]Citizen children of undocumented immigrants.

[e]Immigrant adults using fraudulent documents.

[f]Includes only emergency services to illegal immigrants.

[g]Includes indigent care at the University of California/San Diego, community clinics, and county Public Health services; alcohol and drug abuse; ambulance and paramedics; and uncompensated care.

[h]Includes only costs of incarceration, parole, and obligation bonds for state prisons.

[i]Includes law enforcement, court costs, attorney costs, probation, incarceration/probation/parole, and juvenile justice.

[j]Includes disability insurance, pedestrian improvements, public and low/moderate-income housing.

[k]Excludes K–12.

Table A.4

State and Local Studies of Costs (Dollars) of Immigration: Per-Capita Revenues by Source of Revenue

	Studies					
Source of Revenue	Los Angeles, Co., ISD,[a] 1992	Los Angeles Co.,[a] Clark and Passel,[a] 1994	CA State,[b] Romero, Chang, and Parker, 1994	San Diego,[b] Parker & Rea, 1993	New Jersey State,[c] King, 1994	New Jersey Local,[c] King, 1994
Income tax						
State			37	10	174	
Sales tax						
State			239	114	63	
Local	2	2				
Property tax[d]						
Local	58	121				348
Excise tax (alcohol and tobacco)			37	11	34	
Gasoline tax			34	6		
Vehicle license and registration			48	10	38	
Lottery			35	7		
State unemployment				67		0
Employment training tax				2		
State disability insurance				48		
Employee tax offset by payroll taxes paid				-6		
Public utility tax						60
Inheritance tax					2	
Business/personal property tax					13	
Realty transfer tax					3	
Total	60	123	430	268	327	408

SOURCE: See list of references for full citations of studies.

NOTE: A blank indicates the item was not included. Individual items may not add to totals because of rounding.

[a] Average figures for all immigrants who entered the country after 1980.

[b] Average figures for illegal immigrants only.

[c] Average figures for all immigrants aged 65 or less as of 1980.

[d] All property taxes assumed to be paid by owners of property.

Center for Immigration Studies, *The Costs of Immigration: Assessing a Conflicted Issue*, Book Grounder, No. 2-94, September 1994.

Clark, Rebecca L., et al., *Fiscal Impacts of Undocumented Aliens: Selected Estimates for Seven States*, Washington, D.C.: The Urban Institute, UI/PR-94-1, September 1994.

Clark, Rebecca L., and Jeffrey S. Passel, *How Much Do Immigrants Pay in Taxes? Evidence from Los Angeles County*, Washington, D.C.: The Urban Institute, PRIP-UI-26, August 1993.

DaVanzo, Julie, Jennifer Hawes-Dawson, R. Burciaga Valdez, and Georges Vernez, *Surveying Immigrant Communities: Policy Imperatives and Technical Challenges*, Santa Monica, Calif.: RAND, MR-247-FF, 1994.

Ehrenberg, Ronald, and Robert S. Smith, *Modern Labor Economics*, New York: Harper-Collins, 1991.

Fix, Michael, and Jeffrey S. Passel, *Immigration and Immigrants: Setting the Record Straight*, Washington, D.C.: The Urban Institute, 1994.

Huddle, Donald, *The Costs of Immigration*, Washington, D.C.: Carrying Capacity Network, 1993.

King, Vanessa E., "An Investigation of the Fiscal Impacts of Immigrants in New Jersey," in Thomas J. Espenshade, ed., *A Stone's Throw from Ellis Island: Economic Implications of Immigration to New Jersey*, University Press of America, 1994.

Liu, Lin C., *IRCA's State Legalization Impact Assistance Grants (SLIAG): Early Implementation*, Santa Monica, Calif.: RAND, N-3270-FF, 1991.

Los Angeles County Internal Services Division (ISD), *Impact of Undocumented Persons and Other Immigrants on Costs, Revenues and Services in Los Angeles County*, Los Angeles County, November 6, 1992.

North, David, and Marion Houston, *The Characteristics and Role of Illegal Aliens in the U.S. Labor Market: An Exploratory Study*, Washington, D.C.: Linton and Company, 1976.

Parker, Richard A., and Louis M. Rea, *Illegal Immigration in San Diego County: An Analysis of Costs and Revenues*, Report to the California State Senate Special Committee on Border Issues, California Legislature, September 1993.

Passel, Jeffrey S., *Immigrants and Taxes: A Reappraisal of Huddle's "The Cost of Immigrants,"* Washington, D.C.: The Urban Institute, PRIP-UI-29, January 1994.

Romero, Philip J., Andrew J. Chang, and Theresa Parker, *Shifting the Costs of a Failed Federal Policy: The Net Fiscal Impact of Illegal Immigrants in California*, Sacramento: Governor's Office of Planning and Research, State of California, September 1994.

Rothman, Eric, and Thomas Espenshade, "Fiscal Impacts of Immigration to the United States," *Population Index* 58(3); pp. 381–415, Fall 1992.

U.S. General Accounting Office, *Illegal Aliens: Assessing Estimates of Financial Burden on California*, Washington, D.C.: U.S. Government Printing Office, GAO/HEHS-95-22, November 1994.

U.S. General Accounting Office, *Illegal Aliens: National Net Cost Estimates Vary Widely*, Washington, D.C.: U.S. Government Printing Office, GAO/HEHS-95-133, July 1995.

Vernez, Georges, Needed: A Federal Role in Helping Communities Cope with Immigration, Santa Monica, Calif.: RAND, RP-177, 1993.